WORLD HERITAGE
RAINFOREST

PANOSCAPES
PETER LIK

WILDLIFE PHOTOGRAPHY & TEXT
MIKE PROCIV & MIKE TRENERRY

WILDERNESS PRESS

Front Cover: Daintree National Park
Back Cover: Dainty Treefrog
Title Page: Mossman Gorge National Park
Intro Page: Barron Falls, Kuranda

ISBN 0 646 27968 8
®Panoscapes is a registered trademark of Peter Lik Panoramic Photography.
©Wilderness Press 1996   BK 02

Published by Wilderness Press, an imprint of Peter Lik Photography Pty Ltd.
PO BOX 2529 Cairns Queensland 4870 Australia
PH: (070) 313790   FAX: (070) 313750

To my lovely wife Jude for all her hard work.

CONTENTS

3  Our Magnificent Rainforests

19  Mysterious Jungles - Low land Forests

37  Shrouded in Clouds - High land Rainforest

55 Our Rare and Ancient Heritage

Our Magnificent Rainforests

Rainforests have the richest bounty of life on our planet. They are shaded environments, often with towering trees, heavy rain and splashes of vibrant colour in a sea of greenery. The air is humid and temperatures remain much more stable daily and seasonally, than in any other type of forest. Sometimes described as the earth's lungs, rainforests help supply oxygen and consume a vast amount of carbon dioxide. A large proportion of the world's medicines, food plants (such as fruits and nuts) and many raw products owe their origins to these forests. It is likely that the fate of humanity is linked to the fate of the rainforest.

In Australia, there is only a tiny area of rainforest scattered in a series of patches near the coast. If all of this continent's rainforests were compacted into one square block, it would only be about 140km by 140km, or much less than 1% of Australia's land area. In spite of this small area, well over two-thirds of Australia's ferns, bats and butterfly species live in the rainforest and they are often the most spectacular types. Nearly one half of Australia's bird and plant species are also found in the rainforest, as well as an array of reptiles, frogs and freshwater fish. The diversity of insects and flowering plants are also very high in Australia's rainforest, compared to any other kind of habitat .Rainforest often grows on infertile soil. Fast recycling of dead material is an essential part of a very tight nutrient budget. Decomposers like fungi and small soil animals have the job of making nutrients from wood and dead leaves available for plants to use again quickly.

The world's rainforests may give us clean air and water, house the biggest collection of life on earth, and provide food and medicines yet we have put them under siege. Ideas that these places are dark havens for vermin and should be made to 'pay their way' instead of lying idle, are attitudes that are a hangover from less enlightened times. Only if enough people appreciate the values of these special places will the rainforests be saved.

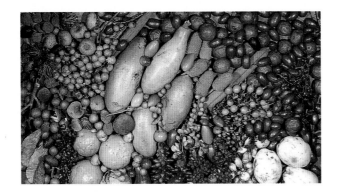

*R*ainforest bats range in size from one quarter the size of a mouse to more than one metre in wing span and one kilogram in weight. They eat huge quantities of insects, nectar and fruit. Bats are amongst the most abundant of the mammals, and two very different and unrelated kinds of bats exist in the rainforest. In one group are the flying foxes, blossom bats and tube-nosed bats. They are big-eyed fruit and nectar feeders which, have no sonar and their closest relatives are primates. Because this group of bats pollinate flowers and spread seeds, they are vital for rainforest health and regeneration. The other bats are the better known smaller species with small eyes, sonar for finding food and their way about. They live in caves and tree hollows. Insects are the main food of these bats.

4

Top left: Rainforest fruits.   *The Tubed Nose Bat.*

The Common Brushtail Possum is the most familiar of the Brushtails.

Primitive forests in the Grand Canyon, Blue Mountains, NSW.

Black bean seed pod and leaf litter.

Bracket Fungi are long-lived and colonise hard timber.

The swift and agile Striped Possum. Its favourite food is wood boring grubs which are extracted from branches with chiselling incisor teeth and extra long probing middle fingers.

Purple Crowned Pigeon.

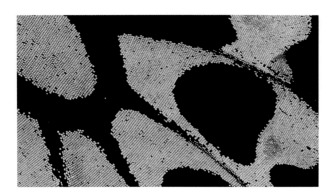

Australia's largest butterfly - Cairns' Birdwing.

The overwhelming green of the forest is broken by the vivid advertising colours of rainforest flowers, fungi, insects and birds. Bright colours attract birds and butterflies to fruit and flowers. Male birds and some insects may use their colours to impress the females. Bright colours can also act as a warning signal to potential enemies. Poisonous and distasteful insects and mushrooms are often bright red, orange or yellow. Some well camouflaged insects, suddenly display boldly marked eye spots or patches of vivid colour (which are normally hidden) to frighten predators when they are disturbed.

Ulysses butterfly flaunts its electric blue wings in tropical North Queensland, Australia.

12 *Natural Arch, Springbrook National Park, Queensland.*

Millaa Millaa Falls surrounded by a natural amphitheatre on the Atherton Tableland. 13

The Waterfall Frog is almost extinct.

Male Red Eyed Tree Frog in a romantic mood.

Dainty Tree Frog.

More than a quarter of Australia's frogs live in the rainforest. These ancient amphibians belong to four families including the tree frogs, southern frogs, the Wood Frog and the tiny microhylid frogs. Three of the best known and most interesting groups of frogs are the Green Tree Frogs, the Barred Frogs and the rainforest stream specialist frogs. Sadly during the 1980s and 1990s fourteen species of stream frogs in Queensland experienced drastic population declines. Seven of these may have become extinct as they can no longer be found in the wild. After a history of more than 160 million years, the disappearance and decline of frogs is continuing worldwide at an alarming rate.

Dainty Tree Frog.

The changing moods of Australia's rainforests.

Moonlight storm provides rain, the lifeblood of the forest. Rainforests need a minimum of 1200mm per annum and can receive more than 11,000mm of rain in one year.

17

18   *Cape Tribulation - a unique meeting of World Heritage areas; tropical rainforest and the Great Barrier Reef.*

Mysterious Jungles – Low Land Rainforests

Low land rainforests present the typical image of "steamy jungles" characterised by large leafed foliage, prickly and strangling vines, broad leafed palms and giant trees with buttressed or aerial roots.

This rainforest type is mainly tropical and coastal in distribution, only occurring in the wettest places where the rainfall is between 1600mm and 5000mm per year. The forest is often structured in layers, each providing a habitat for different plants and animals.

Where the forest canopy is sheltered from the buffeting of strong winds and cyclones, the foliage interlocks, blocking all but the occasional beams of light from penetrating to the forest floor. The forest floor is usually open with a covering of leaf litter and occasional fungi, logs, ferns, shrubs and seedlings.

Where the canopy is opened by destructive weather, or a tree falling, light floods into forest gaps and stimulates a rush of growth from seedlings and vines that may have been lying dormant for many years.

Along gullies and creek banks, there are dense tangles of vines and climbers like a network of hanging ropes reaching up to the canopy.

Branches which receive enough light are festooned with dense cushions of mosses, ferns and orchids, while the stream flood zone contains dense stands of palms and some the world's largest ferns.

Lowland forests are the home of many secretive animals. Brightly coloured birds and butterflies can been seen by day, but darkness sees the emergence of "nightshift" which includes many mammals, frogs, spiders and insects.

The endangered cassowary and the fruit bats consume a wide range of forest fruits, and may carry the seeds a great distance before dropping them. This assists the trees by dispersing seeds in every direction. Their role in the regeneration of plants, and contribution to the health of the forest is so vital, that these animals are known as 'keystone' species.

Licuala fan palms - endemic to North Queensland rainforests.

Previous page: Early morning Cape Tribulation.

The beautiful green python is very rare in Australia. It spends much of its time in rainforest trees hunting for birds and bats.

A Centipede is showing its fangs in a threatening display.

Stinkhorn Fungus

Big compound eyes of giant Longicorn Beetle.

24

The Ring-Tailed Gecko can grow to more than 30cm long and hunts at night around the forest floor.

Terrace Falls in the Blue Mountains, cascades over thirteen tiers.

Buff Breasted Paradise Kingfisher

Flowers of a rainforest vine.

Rainbow Lorikeets screech through the treetops in their quest for nectar from a flame tree.

27

Malay Apple found in Cape York.

With colours like corals and fish of the Great Barrier Reef, the flowers are the jewels of the forest. Blossoms of all shapes, sizes and colours may be seen in the treetops, hanging from vines near the forest floor, along streams and even on tree trunks. Cauliflory is the name for flowers on tree trunks, where they are more protected and rely on different types of animals for pollination. White and pale yellow flowers with a strong sweet night aroma, are designed to attract bats and moths to their offering of nectar. Brightly coloured flowers are usually pollinated by a range of birds and insects during the day. Many of the orchids have beautiful flowers with big showy petals, whereas the trees in the same family as Eucalypts (Myrtacae) have flowers with tiny petals and colourful well developed stamens.

Previous Page: The sparkling waters of Mossman Gorge.

The tiny Queensland blossom bat enjoys a meal of mistletoe nectar.

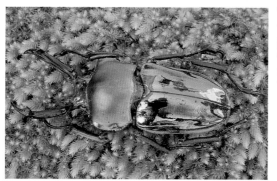

The metallic gloss of a Muellers Stag Beetle.

$\mathcal{I}$nsects are the biggest success story in nature. They've been around for hundreds of millions of years, and there are probably more species of insects than all other animal species combined and perhaps all plant species! There are so many kinds of beetles alone that if all the species were placed in separate matchboxes (some wouldn't fit), which were stacked and balanced end on end, the tower would be taller than Mt. Everest! Insects are the most important agricultural pests, the major pollinators of flowers, and its almost certain that insects will remain long after humans have gone.

Orange Cluster Bugs bright colours warn birds of their foul smell and taste.

31

The magnificent Zillie Falls on the Atherton Tableland surrounded by lush jungle vegetation.

Rain - the lifeblood of all of our forests.

Misty morning in the Otway Ranges, Victoria.

Cup Fungi - less than half the size of a fingernail

Clustering white Agaric Mushrooms.

Red "Velvet" Agaric Mushrooms.

Fungi are the great decomposers and recyclers of nature. Their hair-like filaments invade dead plant matter, and are sometimes parasitic on tree roots. Just about every square centimetre of rainforest soil has fungi filaments. By breaking down organic material so plants can re-use the nutrients, fungi help rainforests to grow on very poor soil. It is the fruiting body (reproductive organs) of fungi that we know as mushrooms, toadstools, bracket fungi and puff-balls. Rainforest fungi may have dazzling colours and bizarre shapes. Slugs, snails, cassowaries, rat kangaroos and insects feed on fungi but many brightly coloured species are poisonous to people and other animals. The incredible stinkhorns are foul smelling, net covered fungi that pop-up after heavy rain.

God's Rays - Dorrigo National Park - NSW.

Mountains shrouded in mist, Dorrigo National Park, NSW.

Shrouded in Clouds - High Land Rainforests

Often shrouded in mist and draped with mosses and ferns, highland and cooler rainforests are amongst the most ancient on earth. From the extremely diverse high altitude wet tropics rainforest to the simpler Tasmanian rainforest, these areas share many common features, even though they are spread over 3,000km. Closely related lizards, birds, snakes, spiny crayfish, primitive stream insects, possums and wallabies are confined to these widely separated places. The same is true for the flora such as ferns and flowering plants, showing that in the long distant past these rainforests were once connected during a period when the climate was cooler and wetter.

Australia's rainiest sites are in the highland rainforests. Some areas are known to receive more than 8 metres of rain each year and have more than 200 rainy days annually. Incredibly, single day rainfalls may sometimes exceed 1000mm. Combined with cloud drip which is regularly experienced, these places can be extremely wet environments. This is reflected in the luxuriance of plant growth, drip tips on leaves, land breeding frogs and in the abundance of plants perched in or clinging to the trees. Like the lowland tropical rainforest, there may be vines, buttressed trees, flowers borne on tree trunks and strangler figs, but these features are less obvious and less common. Leaves are smaller and the wildlife is different. Many species are restricted to the cooler rainforests, and sometimes to just small parts of it.

Of all Australia's natural areas, these forests are amongst the most visually pleasing and biologically important. Even without the opportunity to visit these places, Australians and visitors should be pleased and proud to know that they exist in this country.

38   *Resurrection Plant living on Mt Koolmoon near Tully Qld, change from green in the wet season to bright orange in the hot and dry spring months.*

Monkey Spider

Mt. Peiter Botte, one of the highest peaks in Daintree National Park. 39

Opposite Page: Tchupalla Falls - One of the most picturesque waterfalls in the Palmerston section of Wooroonooran National Park, North Queensland.

Brown Lemuroid Possum, a climbing marsupial of the highest mountains.

42 *Early morning mist through tree ferns Sherbrooke Forest, Victoria.*

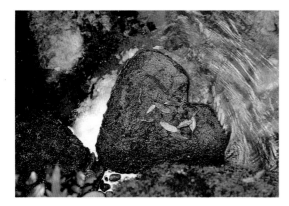

Nature's heart of the rainforest.

Cairns' Birdwing - Australia's largest Butterfly.

Red Cheeked Marsupial Mouse shelters in a hollow. 43

44 *The cool clear water and mossy ferny creeks of Mt. Lewis provide home for a large and varied community of wildlife.*

Temperate rainforest of the Otway Ranges, Victoria.

The rare Golden Bower Bird.

The Satin Bower Bird decorates its bower.

47

48　*Nandroya Falls - Wooroonooran National Park -　Atherton Tableland Queensland.*

Daintree River Ringtail Possum.

*A*ustralian rainforests are the home of fourteen species of possums. They are a varied range of tree dwelling nocturnal marsupials. The five kinds of ringtails include the familiar Common Ringtail, the beautifully marked Green Ringtail and the rare Daintree Ringtail. A prehensile tail enhances their ability to climb. Brushtails are larger with bigger ears, and two species have a number of different colour forms. The much more agile striped possum looks like a sleek skunk. Eastern and long-tailed pygmy possums are tiny, almost elfin species with secretive habits. The wet tropics upland rainforest is the richest for possums with nine species. The very distinctive Coppery Brushtail and the spectacular white Lemuroid Possums are also found in this region, but are only considered to be varieties of more widespread possum species.

Common Ringtail Possum on the nightshift in the rainforest. 49

Upper Wentworth Falls, Blue Mountains, NSW.

Katoomba Falls, Blue Mountains, NSW.

Orange Cruiser Butterfly.

Situated only 65km west of Sydney lies the panoramic *Blue Mountains National Park*, the fourth largest National Park in New South Wales, covering an area of 216,000 hectares. The deep gorges and sheer rockfaces provide incredible vistas of some of the world's most magnificent waterfalls, plunging over 100m. Some of the famous waterfalls include:- *Bridal Veil falls*, *Wentworth falls* and *Katoomba falls*. Rainforest pockets are scattered through valleys in the wettest areas.

Nocturnal Papuan Frogmouth.

Green Ring-Tailed Possum.

Embracing Red-Eyed Tree Frogs.

Antarctic Beech trees in Lamington National Park, south east Queensland approximately 3,000 years old.

Our Rare and Ancient Heritage

Tens of millions of years ago, Australia broke away from Antarctica and the other southern continents that made up the supercontinent Gondwanaland. It took with it a share of the ancient rainforests and their inhabitants. Scattered in small pockets along the east coast of Australia and Tasmania are the remnants of these great forests. With some Asian and New Guinean rainforest 'mixing' in the North as a result of land bridges to Asia during the low sea levels of ice-ages, these surviving Australian rainforest areas are like windows to the past. They are living museums and are the longest continually rainforested places on earth. To be found here is an astonishing assortment of 'living fossils', including the largest collection of primitive flowering plants on Earth, the most ancient of song birds and the ancestral lineages of many groups of animals and plants.

Even before European people arrived in Australia, rainforest covered a mere one five hundredth of the land surface of this continent. Most of the rainforest has been cleared for grazing and agriculture, especially on the rare fertile soils, coastal plains and flatter tablelands where the best rainforest was found. Logging removed the centuries-old giants, plant and animal pest species invaded much of the surviving rainforest, and development still threatens to further erode these forests.

More than 500 species of plants in the wet tropics region alone are rare and threatened. As recently as the 1980s and 1990s fourteen of Queensland's rainforest frogs became critically endangered, and seven of them are probably extinct.

Because Australia's rainforests are so important, and are recognised internationally as treasures of the natural world, several rainforest areas between Tasmania and North Queensland have been placed on the World Heritage list. This ensures the protection of these magnificent forests so future generations will be not be denied the chance to experience them.

A majestic old Fig Tree stands proud in the forest.

Rare Forest Fruits.

A Rare Pink Hyacinth Orchid.

Dark Lemuroid Possum and Baby - creatures of the night.

Mountain Mist Frog may now be extinct.

Colourful Mt. Lewis Spiny Crayfish.

The Cassowary is the world's second largest bird, growing up to 2 metres tall.

Boyd's Forest Dragon's fearsome appearance belies its placid nature. An expert climber, it may drop to the ground on unweary insects. 59

The strange and rarely seen Chameleon Gecko has the face of an alien. It is a survivor of a bygone era.

Lumholtz Tree Kangaroo.

𝓔xtinction is forever! Whilst it's true that no species lasts forever, the world's plants and animals are disappearing at an unprecedented rate. Perhaps not since the fall of the dinosaurs more than 60 million years ago has the Earth lost so many species in such a short time. Humans have replaced forests with agriculture and wild animals with domestic stock. We have polluted our planet and spread pests and diseases. Every year the World loses over one thousand species of 'larger' plants and animals, and every year this number increases. Nature enriches our lives, and the crisis the natural World is suffering should be of concern to everybody. All species should have the 'right to exist'. We have the means to rescue many of them from extinction for which we are responsible.

Perhaps Australia's cutest animal the extremely rare White Lemuroid Possum.

"My total dedication and obsession with photography has taken me on journeys into many remarkable areas throughout Australia. I captured this collection of "Panoscapes" on a range of specialist 6cm x 17cm panoramic cameras. This format enabled me to portray the sheer expanse of living museums of rainforests, and other World Heritage areas on film because of the wider field of view as seen by the human eye. Upon viewing these images I am sure you will share with me the tranquility and solitude I experienced deep in the heart of these awesome World Heritage sites."

Wilderness Warehouse combines the scientific technical and artistic skills of two professional wildlife photographers. Mike Prociv commenced wildlife photography whilst working as a National Park Ranger. He established and manages Wetro-pics Photgraphic Library which is quickly becoming recognised as one of the best collections of Wet Tropics ecology and scenery. In 1994, Mike won an African Safari as first prize in "The Australian" Wildlife Photographic Competition. Michael Trenerry training and experience as an ecologist and zoologist has provided insights and photographic opportunities seldom afforded to other photographers. Michael's unique style and technical excellence have been widely acclaimed over the past decade.

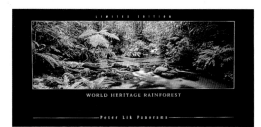

Limited Edition Poster 600mm x 1000mm @ $29.95
Refer to page 44.

White Lemuroid Possum

***Rainforest
Creatures
Posters***
410mm x 547mm
@ $19.95

Northern Red-eyed Tree Frog

Posters delivered free anywhere in Australia.
Please call or fax us for a brochure on our full product range including - books, posters, greeting cards and postcards.
Ph: (070) 313790   Fax: (070) 313750